INSIDE THE REFORMATION

The Times That Changed the World

CONCORDIA PUBLISHING HOUSE · SAINT LOUIS

© iStockphoto.com

Compiled by Mark S. Sengele

The quotation on page 44 is from pages 112–13 of Luther's Works from The American Edition, vol. 32 © 1958 Muhlenberg Press. Used by permission of Augsburg Fortress.

The quotation on page 63 is from page 358 of Luther's Works from The American Edition, vol. 49 © 1972 Augsburg Fortress, used by permission of the publisher.

Endsheet art: © Shutterstock, Inc.

Unless otherwise noted, Scripture quotations are from the ESV Bible® (The Holy Bible, English Standard Version®), copyright © 2001 by Crossway Bibles, a publishing ministry of Good News Publishers. Used by permission. All rights reserved.

This publication may be available in braille, in large print, or on cassette tape for the visually impaired. Please allow 8 to 12 weeks for delivery. Write to Lutheran Blind Mission, 7550 Watson Rd., St. Louis, MO 63119-4409; call toll-free 1-888-215-2455; or visit the Web site: www.blindmission.org

Library of Congress Cataloging-in-Publication Data

Inside the Reformation / [compiled Mark S. Sengele].

  p. cm.

  ISBN 978-0-7586-3120-6

1. Reformation--Juvenile literature. I. Sengele, Mark.

BR308.I57 2012

270.6--dc23   2011044779

Manufactured in China

1   2   3   4   5   6   7   8   9   10
21 20 19 18 17 16 15 14 13 12

CONTENTS

© Shutterstock, Inc.

© iStockphoto.com

© Ray Roper/iStockphoto.com

© iStockphoto.com

Middle Ages

The Middle Ages (or medieval period) lasted from about AD 400 to 1500, roughly from the fall of Rome to the Renaissance. During this time period, much of Europe became more populated, and many of the countries we know today took shape. Most people in Europe lived in a feudal society, where wealthy landowners leased part of their land to knights, who in turn leased smaller parcels of land to poor peasants. The vast majority of people were very poor and depended on the knights and landowners for protection. The structure of society gradually began to change as explorers found new routes for trade with countries in the East and more individuals sought to buy goods and materials rather than producing them on their own.

Renaissance

The Renaissance spans around 1300 to 1700, overlapping the Middle Ages. Most experts say the Renaissance began in Florence, Italy, in the late Middle Ages. The Renaissance brought about new interest in the arts and sciences and a return to classical learning.

Reformation

The Reformation spans the years 1517, when Martin Luther published his Ninety-five Theses, until 1648, when the Treaty of Westphalia brought an end to the religious wars in Europe.

© Derek Dammann/iStockphoto.com

The religious and cultural influence of the Holy Roman Empire spread far beyond central Europe. This fresco from the Cathedral Church of Saint Peter in Exeter, England is typical of the art style popularized by the empire during the medieval period.

© Renars Jurkovskis/ Shutterstock, Inc.

This coin bears the coat of arms of Ferdinand I, who served briefly as emperor of the Holy Roman Empire 1558–1564. His more important work occurred at the Diet of Augsburg, where he worked out a compromise that allowed the Catholic believers and the followers of Luther to live together peacefully. Eventually, he replaced his brother, Holy Roman Emperor Charles V.

This woodcut is of Holy Roman Emperor Maximilian II (1527–1576). He was the son of Ferdinand I and served as emperor from 1564 to 1576. While remaining verbally loyal to the Roman Catholic Church, Maximilian II granted liberty to the Lutheran princes in Germany. At the same time, he refused to enforce the new rules outlined by the Catholic Church leaders at the Council of Trent.

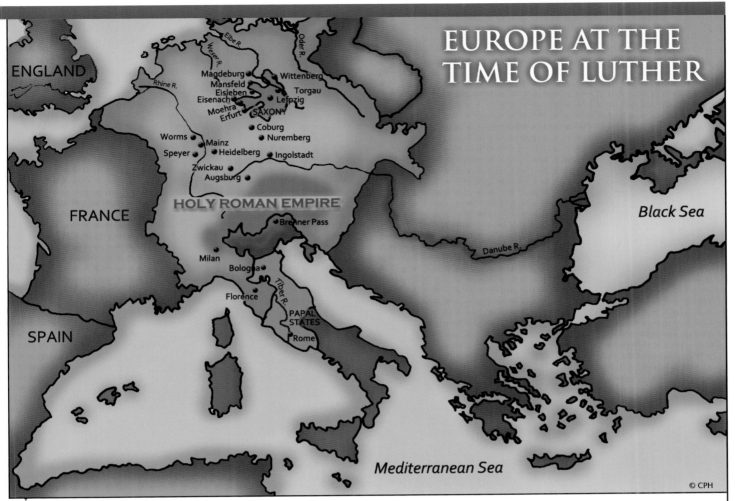

EUROPE AT THE TIME OF LUTHER

ENGLAND

Elbe R.
Weser R.
Oder R.
Rhine R.
Magdeburg
Mansfeld
Wittenberg
Eisleben
Torgau
Eisenach
Leipzig
Moehra
SAXONY
Erfurt
Coburg
Worms
Nuremberg
Mainz
Speyer
Heidelberg
Ingolstadt
Zwickau
Augsburg

FRANCE

HOLY ROMAN EMPIRE

Brenner Pass

Black Sea

Danube R.

Milan
Bologna
Tiber R.
Florence
PAPAL STATES
Rome

SPAIN

Mediterranean Sea

© CPH

While the title "Holy Roman Empire" might make you think of ancient Rome, the real story is quite different. The Holy Roman Empire encompassed a large area, including much of modern-day Germany, Austria, Switzerland, Hungary, and Luxembourg. These predominantly German-speaking countries and city-states formed a loose alliance under an emperor elected by the local noblemen and approved by the Roman Catholic Church. Emperors had little real power to control the often-divided local rulers and villages. Napoleon finally abolished the Holy Roman Empire in 1806, but the Austro-Hungarian Empire continued until 1918. Meanwhile, Prussia managed to organize the separate German states to form the German Empire.

Often called the first Christian emperor, Constantine appears in this Byzantine mosaic along with Justinian and the Virgin Mary with the Christ Child. Constantine and Justinian are portrayed presenting Constantinople and the St. Sophia Basilica to Mary.

Christopher Columbus (1451–1506)

While probably best known for his first voyage in 1492, Columbus actually sailed to the New World on four separate occasions. While Columbus never actually set foot on North America, he explored the Caribbean islands and established several settlements. Throughout his explorations, Columbus was convinced that he was sailing along the east coast of Asia. He never realized the American continents lay between Europe and Asia.

© Sergey Mikhaylov/Shutterstock, Inc.

Vasco da Gama (1460–1524)

Vasco da Gama achieved what Columbus set out to do—to find a water route to India. He accomplished this goal by sailing around the southern tip of Africa at the Cape of Good Hope. Da Gama's initial success led to a second voyage to India with even more ships before settling down in Portugal to marry and raise a family.

© Sergey Mikhaylov/Shutterstock, Inc.

Francis Drake (1540–1596)

As an explorer, Drake sailed around the world, having successfully navigated Cape Horn at the southern tip of South America and the Cape of Good Hope at the tip of Africa. Drake continued to serve the British crown as he led attacks on Spanish and Portuguese ports. On his final voyage to cut off the Spanish settlements in Panama, Drake fell ill, died, and was buried at sea.

© Sergey Mikhaylov/Shutterstock, Inc.

© Slava Gerj/Shutterstock, Inc.

This historic—but somewhat inaccurate—map celebrates the first exploration of Christopher Columbus. Notice the out-of-proportion shapes of North and South America based on the limited information European explorers and map makers had at the time.

The magnetic compass was invented by the Chinese around the second century BC. Once the compass was introduced to medieval Europe, it became a vital tool for world explorers.

© Shutterstock, Inc.

© Shutterstock, Inc.

Amerigo Vespucci (1454–1512)

A skilled navigator, Vespucci went on at least two, and possibly four, voyages across the Atlantic. He was one of the first explorers to suggest that what Columbus had found was not the coast of Asia, but rather part of a New World. In 1507, a pamphlet was published suggesting the New World be named in Vespucci's honor: America.

© Sergey Mikhaylov/Shutterstock, Inc.

Ferdinand Magellan (1480–1521)

Like Columbus, Magellan's explorations were funded by the king of Spain. This Portuguese explorer set out to sail around the world. He discovered a new route around South America, now called the Strait of Magellan. The expedition faced many challenges, including the death of Magellan while in the Philippines. Of the five ships and nearly three hundred men who started the journey, only one ship and eighteen men survived.

© Sergey Mikhaylov/Shutterstock, Inc.

Hernán Cortés (1485–1547)

The Spanish explorer Cortés spent most of his time in Mexico and Central America. Among his many accomplishments, Cortés was responsible for defeating the Aztecs in Mexico and establishing Mexico City as a European city.

© Sergey Mikhaylov/Shutterstock, Inc.

© iStockphoto.com

Leonardo da Vinci was a man of incredible talent. As a painter, sculptor, and inventor, da Vinci never stopped learning and exploring. Da Vinci was left-handed in a time when this was considered the devil's doing. Today, some researchers speculate da Vinci's left-handedness contributed to his creative thinking. Unlike most other fifteenth-century individuals, Leonardo was also a strict vegetarian.

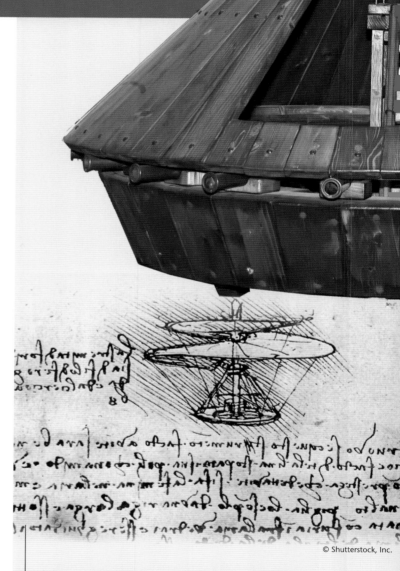

© Shutterstock, Inc.

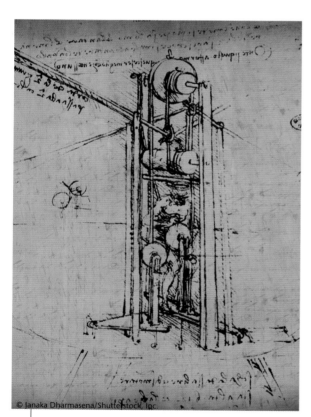

© Janaka Dharmasena/Shutterstock, Inc.

As Leonardo da Vinci learned and studied, he kept a series of notebooks with sketches of ideas and inventions covering four main themes: painting, architecture, mechanical engineering, and anatomy. Gears and pulleys particularly fascinated Leonardo; many of his invention ideas used gears and pulleys to perform tasks.

Da Vinci sketched what he called the helical airscrew. His plan envisioned men running on the circular platform, which would cause the fan to rotate, lifting the machine from the ground. Hundreds of years later, this concept would inspire the modern-day helicopter.

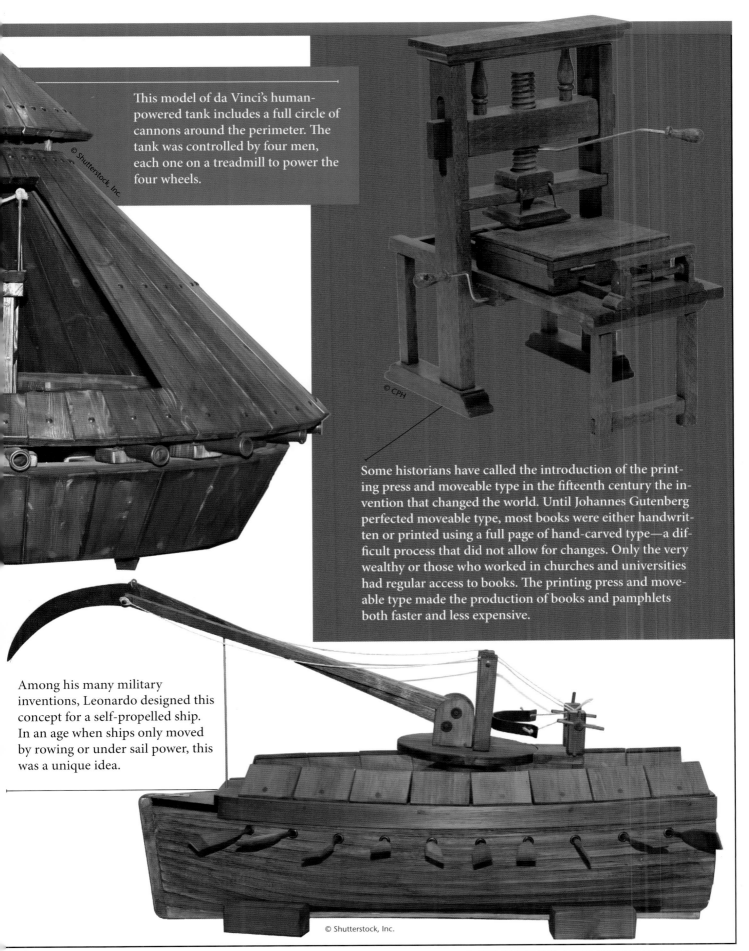

This model of da Vinci's human-powered tank includes a full circle of cannons around the perimeter. The tank was controlled by four men, each one on a treadmill to power the four wheels.

© Shutterstock, Inc.

© CPH

Some historians have called the introduction of the printing press and moveable type in the fifteenth century the invention that changed the world. Until Johannes Gutenberg perfected moveable type, most books were either handwritten or printed using a full page of hand-carved type—a difficult process that did not allow for changes. Only the very wealthy or those who worked in churches and universities had regular access to books. The printing press and moveable type made the production of books and pamphlets both faster and less expensive.

Among his many military inventions, Leonardo designed this concept for a self-propelled ship. In an age when ships only moved by rowing or under sail power, this was a unique idea.

© Shutterstock, Inc.

The tightly packed buildings of the medieval village of Colledimezzo, Italy, include homes, businesses, and churches. Families were crowded together in small apartments. Only the wealthiest families had private homes. Shops and businesses were all within walking distance. The location on a hillside provides safety from enemies. Some cities had a wall surrounding them for additional protection.

This streetscape in Girona, Spain, displays another trait of medieval cities. Because roads were meant only for foot traffic and the cities were sometimes hilly, the builders made use of steps to conquer steep slopes.

na Elisseeva/Shutterstock, Inc.

The narrow streets of Perigueux, Perigorg, France, are typical of cities during the Reformation. Built during the medieval era, these cobbled streets were only intended for pedestrian traffic.

© Shutterstock, Inc.

This illustration of a medieval town shows how buildings were clustered tightly together, often around a public square and adjacent to churches or town buildings.

Plotnikov/Shutterstock, Inc.

The vast salt flats near Mont Saint-Michel provide pasture lands for grazing sheep. Like many medieval cities, the residents lived within the safety of the city walls and natural boundaries but depended on acres of agricultural land nearby for grazing livestock and planting crops.

omas Barrat/Shutterstock, Inc.

Mont Saint-Michel in Brittany, France, was once an islet during high tide, with a land bridge connecting to the rest of the country most of the time. French engineers recently completed a massive project that will restore Mont Saint-Michel's island status. As with many medieval villages, the abbey of Saint-Michel served as the central focus of the island. The remote location protected the residents of Mont Saint-Michel from potential invaders for many years.

Clothing

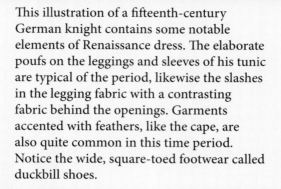

© Steven Wynn/
iStockphoto.com

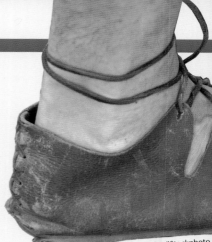

© Werner Münzker/iStockphoto.

This illustration of a fifteenth-century German knight contains some notable elements of Renaissance dress. The elaborate poufs on the leggings and sleeves of his tunic are typical of the period, likewise the slashes in the legging fabric with a contrasting fabric behind the openings. Garments accented with feathers, like the cape, are also quite common in this time period. Notice the wide, square-toed footwear called duckbill shoes.

This elegant dress would only be worn by someone very wealthy. The heavy brocade fabrics and elaborate lace collar along with the patterns of decorative buttons, embroidery, and fine details show the wearer was someone of high status. Take note of the padded poufs at the shoulder, the fitted sleeves, and the floor-length trains at each arm. Clothing of this type not only reflected wealth, but also served as a form of investment. If the family needed money in the future, elegant dresses like this might be sold for a profit.

© Dario Sabljak/Shutterstock, Inc.

© Shutterstock, Inc.

This woman wears a simple dress made of velvet. The lace-up bodice, wide sleeves, and gold braiding add color and style to this outfit. Like most women from this era, she wears a head covering. Most people in this time period only owned one set of clothing. Clothing at this time was typically hand sewn and made specifically for the wearer.

The fitted jerkin or tunic, with its row of small buttons, was a fashion staple for the Renaissance man. Velvet, leather, and brocade were typical fabrics for the jerkin, which was often sleeveless. Men wore tall stockings and leggings with these tunics.

© Shutterstock, Inc.

Here, we see two different styles of shoes. The simple leather shoe on the left was not much more than a piece of leather with laces to tie it securely to the foot. The shoe on the right is an example of the elaborate style a wealthy client might choose.

Fashion historians trace the pointy-toe style to slippers from the Middle East. To make it stand out, the pointed tip would be stuffed with moss, hair, or wool.

© Shutterstock, Inc.

© Cindy England/iStockphoto.com

This bronze disk inlaid with amber would be worn around the waist of a tunic much like a belt would be worn today. This belt could be worn by a man or a woman.

© Marina Kryukova/ Shutterstock, Inc.

© Vladislav Gajic / Shutterstock, Inc.

Like fine clothing, jewelry would only be worn by very wealthy people. This silver ring with engraving demonstrates the skill of the craftsman who made it. Pearls like the ones shown above were among the treasures available in the Far East. Goods like this prompted explorers to find new and shorter trade routes to this part of the world.

The young woman in this portrait wears the latest in Renaissance fashion. Her off-the-shoulder gown with full sleeves and multiple jewelry pieces indicate her family's wealth and status. Another unique part of the painting is the inclusion of a rabbit, often a symbol for love.

Food and Drink

© Shutterstock, Inc.

Noblemen hunted many varieties of game animals to feed their extended households. Common game birds included duck and pheasant. Other game animals included deer and boar. Farmers and even some town dwellers kept chickens, doves, pigs, goats, and beef cattle for meat. Those meats not eaten right away had to be preserved by smoking, potting, or salting. Fresh fish were only common in coastal areas; otherwise, they were pickled, smoked, or salted. The wealthy took pride in serving elaborate banquets with exotic food such as roasted peacock decorated with its own feathers.

© Kelly Cline/iStockphoto.com

Oats and barley were commonly grown grains in this time period. Working-class families depended on these grains for their baking and cooking needs. Both could be ground into flour for making porridges.

© iStockphoto.com

Bread was a food staple during the Reformation. Dark whole grain breads were eaten by most people because wheat flour would be reserved for use in households of noble or wealthy individuals. Before the use of loaf pans, bread came in many shapes, including round or oval loaves formed by hand and baked in a wood-fired oven.

© Amit Erez/iStockphoto.com

The production and consumption of wine and beer was important during this era. Since there was no reliable method of refrigeration, the consumption of milk was limited to what the family cow gave each day (and what was not used for cooking). The purity of water could be questionable, and coffee was virtually unknown. So the use of fermented beverages was quite common.

© Leonid Nyshko/iStockphoto.com

© Shutterstock, Inc.

Covered tankards, like this pewter example, were used for holding beer or ale. Pewter and silver were commonly used for everyday plates and cups in wealthy households. Rough pottery mugs and tankards were used in lower-class families. Everyday meals might be served on stale bread crusts. Common people rarely had forks and spoons; instead, they used their hands to eat.

Honey was readily available as a sweetener rather than the more expensive sugar. Sugar was such an expensive commodity, it was usually kept locked in special sugar chests and used in small quantities.

Wheat was grown during this era, but because it was more difficult and expensive to grow, the use of wheat flour was common only among the very wealthy. The wheat grown by farmers on their small fields helped pay the noblemen who owned the land.

© iStockphoto.com

© Steven Wynn/iStockphoto.com

This lithograph print shows fourteenth-century women gathered in an outdoor setting to visit and play music. Notice the violin and the large, stringed instrument similar to an Autoharp. One woman has a small dog on her lap and another woman holds a bird of prey.

© Ferran Traite Soler/iStockphoto.com

© Kari Hoglund/iStockphoto.com

Music at the time of the Reformation was frequently written by hand. Some highly decorated music scores did exist, but these likely would only be used in a church rather than at home.

The great cathedrals throughout Europe used pipe organs to fill their vast interiors with sound. Each organ was hand built, requiring thousands of moving parts. Playing the organ required two people. The organist played the keys and pedals while manipulating the stops for different sounds. The calcant operated the bellows used to create the air for the pipes.

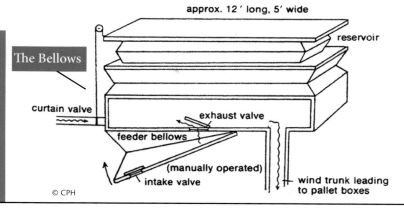

© CPH

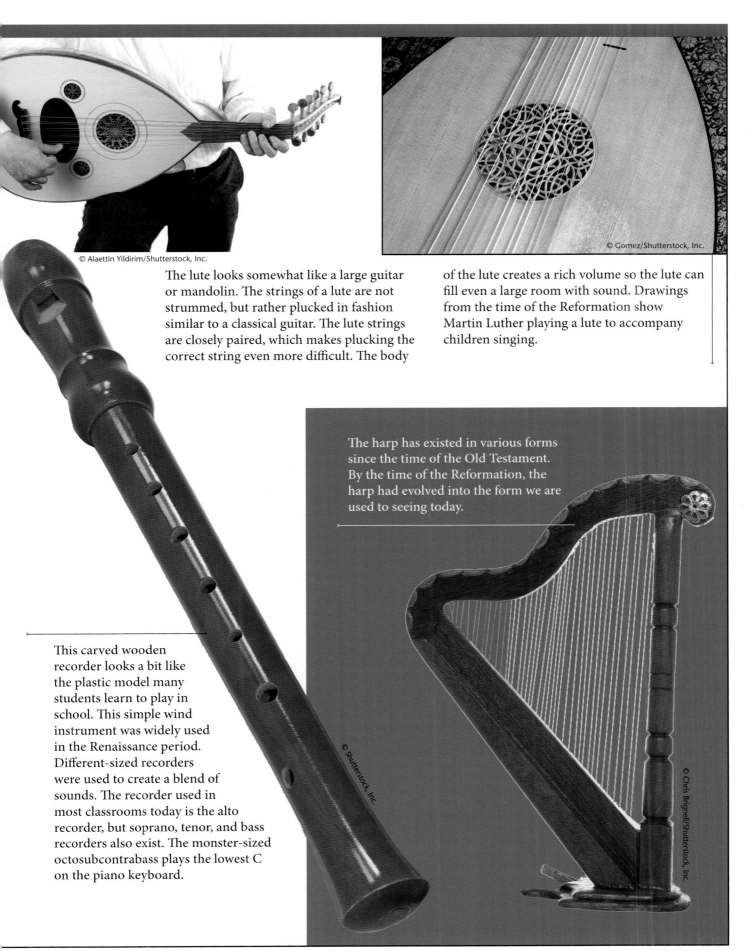

The lute looks somewhat like a large guitar or mandolin. The strings of a lute are not strummed, but rather plucked in fashion similar to a classical guitar. The lute strings are closely paired, which makes plucking the correct string even more difficult. The body of the lute creates a rich volume so the lute can fill even a large room with sound. Drawings from the time of the Reformation show Martin Luther playing a lute to accompany children singing.

© Alaettin Yildirim/Shutterstock, Inc.

© Gomez/Shutterstock, Inc.

The harp has existed in various forms since the time of the Old Testament. By the time of the Reformation, the harp had evolved into the form we are used to seeing today.

This carved wooden recorder looks a bit like the plastic model many students learn to play in school. This simple wind instrument was widely used in the Renaissance period. Different-sized recorders were used to create a blend of sounds. The recorder used in most classrooms today is the alto recorder, but soprano, tenor, and bass recorders also exist. The monster-sized octosubcontrabass plays the lowest C on the piano keyboard.

© Shutterstock, Inc.

© Chris Brignell/Shutterstock, Inc.

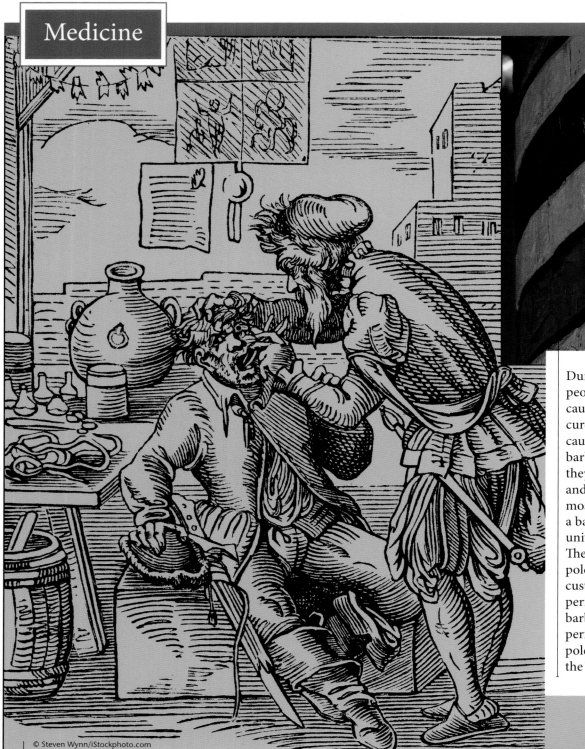

© Steven Wynn/iStockphoto.com

During the medieval period, people thought disease was caused by bad blood. The cure was to intentionally cause bleeding. Medieval barbers not only cut hair, but they also performed bleeding and minor surgery. Because most people could not read, a barber pole became a universal sign for the barber. The red stripe on the barber pole reminded potential customers that barbers also performed bleedings. While barbers today no longer perform surgery, the barber pole is still used to identify the barber shop.

This vintage woodcut shows a surgeon or dentist performing a procedure on a patient. In the Reformation era, a doctor's duties might include surgery, dental work, or making medications.

One of the tools used by the barber or physician to perform bleedings is the leech. Leeches attach themselves to their victim by their mouth parts and draw out blood until their entire body is bloated. Interestingly, some doctors today use leeches to draw out blood pooled near surgical sites.

© Sergey Lukianov/iStockphoto.com

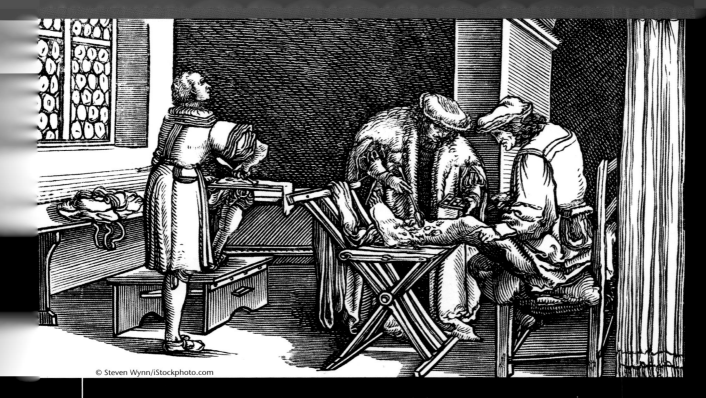

This woodcut by Hans Holbein the Younger (1497–1543) shows a German surgeon operating on a wounded leg. In this time before much use of anesthesia, the patient's pain and suffering was great.

This woodcut shows the interior of a fifteenth-century doctor's home. The patient appears to be receiving medication from the doctor. Not the large books and other symbols of the doctor's status. Only very learned or wealt individuals would ha books at home.

Because books were so expensive to produce during the medieval age, only universities, libraries, or churches had access to books. The very wealthy and priests may have had have a few books in their homes.

Unlike today, not every child in medieval times attended school. Most schools at this time would be connected to universities or the church. Martin Luther started school at a young age. By the time he was fourteen, Luther left home to attend school in a town far from his home. Students were encouraged to beg for coins on the city streets; sometimes, students would sing to get the attention of potential donors.

Children in the Reformation era were educated in various ways. Young girls learned to take care of a future family and household by working alongside their mothers. A boy often learned to follow in his father's career by working with him. Some boys would receive training for a future career through an apprenticeship. An apprentice agreed to work for someone for a certain length of time in exchange for training in that career.

© Ivar Teunissen/iStockphoto.com

If you misbehaved in school during the Renaissance period, you might end up wearing a donkey mask as part of your punishment. The mask was meant to show other students how foolish your behavior was.

Students in the Reformation era would not have used pens or pencils for writing. During this time, writing was done using a feather quill dipped in an inkwell. Students would have to hand cut their quill points using a small knife. Ink was made by boiling or crushing plant galls in a solution of water, wine, or vinegar. The resulting liquid was mixed with iron powder to create ink.

Calligraphy Ink

By the time of the Reformation, as much as one third of the land in Europe was owned by the Roman Catholic Church. Bishops oversaw vast stretches of land for the archbishops and the pope. Common people often became nuns and monks in order to be provided for by the church. Nuns and monks were not allowed to marry; their entire lives were dedicated to serving the church.

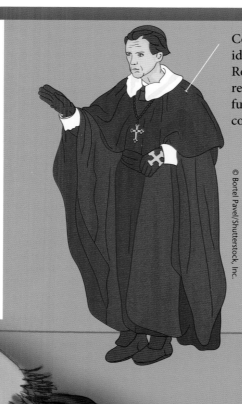

Color plays an important role to help identify the rank of members of the Roman Catholic clergy. Here, the bright red indicates the rank of cardinal. The full, flowing robe and slippers further confirm the wearer's status.

© Bortel Pavel/Shutterstock, Inc.

© Shutterstock, Inc.

When a young man wanted to become a Catholic priest, he went through a series of training steps. A beginner is called a novice. When Martin Luther became a novice, he put on the white robe and black cloak indicating his role. In addition, he received the tonsure, which involved shaving the top of his head.

© CPH

The seal of the papacy contains a number of symbols indicating the role and purpose of the pope. The crossed keys symbolize the keys of Peter. The keys are gold and silver to represent the power of loosing and binding sin. The triple crown (the tiara) represents the pope's three functions as "supreme pastor," "supreme teacher," and "supreme priest." The gold cross on the top of the tiara symbolizes the sovereignty of Jesus.

Numina cœlestem nobis peperere Lutherum,
Nostra diu matus fœcia videre nihil.
Quem si Pontificum crudelis deprimit error,
Non feret iratos impia terra Deos.

In this engraving of Martin Luther as a young priest, you can clearly see his tonsure. Like all priests in his order, Luther would have worn the tonsure throughout his time in the monastery.

This woodcut shows Martin Luther arriving at the Augustinian monastery in Erfurt to beginning his training for the church. Some time earlier, Luther was caught in a violent thunderstorm. He was so frightened for his life, Martin made a promise to Saint Anne that if he could be spared, he would commit his life to the priesthood. Luther later regretted his promise, but he kept his word.

Pilgrimage

© Valetin Casarsa/iStockphoto.com

Pilgrimages to visit holy sites were very common during the Renaissance. People believed they could earn favor with God by visiting certain pilgrimage sites. To accommodate the needs of these pilgrims who traveled on foot, local churches built small roadside chapels where pilgrims could stop to rest and pray on the long routes between towns and villages.

© Oleg Senkov/Shutterstock, Inc.

This statue of a pilgrim on his journey is found near the cathedral in Speyer, Germany. The cathedral lies along a popular pilgrimage route called the Way of Saint James. Pilgrims from across Europe followed this route to visit the relics of the twelve apostles at Santiago de Compostela in Spain. As shown in the sculpture, pilgrims traveled the route barefoot as a symbol of their repentance.

This woodcut from the time of the Reformation shows pilgrims arriving at the Church of the Beautiful Virgin at Regensburg, Germany. Many of the pilgrims lie on the ground at the foot of the statue of Mary, believing they could somehow earn favor with God through their actions.

Some of the monks in Luther's order were involved in a controversy. They sent Luther and another monk to Rome in order to get an official ruling from the Vatican on their dispute. This ancient map of Rome shows some of the sights Martin Luther may have seen when he went on his pilgrimage to Rome in 1510. The Vatican occupied the very heart of the city. Martin planned to use any extra time in Rome to visit the many relics found there. After the six-week trip on foot, Luther fell to the ground and cried, "Greetings to you, holy Rome!"

ROMA.

© Pablo Ficola/iStockphoto.com

© Mikael Hjerpe//iStockphoto.com

© iStockphoto.com

During this time, streets in towns and villages were paved with cobblestones. While this cobblestone street might seem really rough compared to streets today, this was much better than the alternative. Once outside of town, most roads would be dirt trails from place to place. The cobblestone pavement made it possible for roads to be used all year. Without pavement, the dirt roads could become almost impassible during heavy rains and in the early spring.

One of the fastest ways to travel long distances was by ship. Most large towns were located along lakes or rivers to make travel by water possible. While faster than walking, ship travel could be very expensive as well as potentially dangerous. Ships at this time had shared cabins or just an open cargo space for both merchandise and passengers. Everyone crowded together to share the meager supplies available.

When you traveled during the Renaissance and Reformation, it involved a great deal of planning and time. Unlike today, you did not just go away for a weekend. Long trips could take weeks or even months. For those who could travel by wagon or ship, it meant packing for these extended time periods. People during this time did not have luggage like today, so they used large chests or trunks like this one.

Both open and enclosed horse-drawn carriages were only available to the wealthy or royalty. While faster than walking, horse-powered transportation still could take a long time to travel between towns and cities.

Relics

For many years, the Roman Catholic Church taught that by looking at, praying over, or kissing the relics of saints or Christ Himself, you could earn rewards toward heaven. Relics included things like thorns from Jesus' crown, slivers of wood from the cross, a nail from the cross, crumbs of bread left from the feeding of the five thousand, branches from the burning bush of Moses, and many more. The true identity of relics was hard to verify or cloaked in mystery.

Courtesy: Yale University

Sometimes, the reliquary was designed to take the appearance of an angel or the saint. This figural bust of an unknown saint made approximately 1310–1325 comes from Cologne, Germany. Most reliquary busts were made of metal, but this example is carved from wood, gessoed (coated with plaster and water), and then painted.

© Mirek Hejnicki/Shutterstock, Inc.

The San Paolo fouri le Mura chapel in Rome shows how some churches gathered numerous relics together in one place. By the time Luther visited Rome, there were thousands of relics to be viewed, touched, and prayed over.

© Zvonimir Atletic/Shutterstock, Inc.

This decorative box built into the wall of a church is called a reliquary. Reliquaries are designed to hold sacred objects associated with a saint or Jesus. Notice the row of angels across the top of the reliquary and the carving of Jesus on the cross in the center panel.

© Rostislav Ageev/Shutterstock, Inc.

This Eastern Orthodox Church in Thessaloniki, Macedonia, Greece, preserves these relics of Agios Dimitrios (Saint Demetrius). The church is built where Demetrius was believed to have been martyred. Notice how the walls of the room are decorated with paintings resembling icons typically associated with the Orthodox Church.

Courtesy: Yale University

This enameled reliquary from approximately 1220 is covered with porcelain images of angels. The decorative box would have held items associated with saints.

In 2010, German artist Ottmar Hörl installed eight hundred copies of the famous sculpture of Martin Luther in the market square of Wittenberg. The installation entitled "Martin Luther: Here I Stand . . ." was named for the famous quote Luther spoke at the Diet of Worms.

© Ottmar Hörl - installation "Martin Luther: Here I Stand . . ." - Wittenberg / Germany (2011) - photo: Christoph Busse

Martin Luther became a professor at the University of Wittenberg on October 19, 1512. He would hold this position for the remaining thirty-four years of his life. This sculpture of Luther stands in the city square of Wittenberg, Germany, which became the center of the Reformation movement.

© Ralf Gosch/iStockphoto.com

On October 31, 1517, Martin Luther changed the history of the world when he posted his Ninety-five Theses on the door of Castle Church in Wittenberg. The tower of Castle Church—also called All Saints Church—still stands over Wittenberg today.

An overhead view of the square in Wittenberg, Germany, shows the eight hundred copies of the Luther statue installed by artist Ottmar Hörl. Wittenberg has not changed much in the last five hundred years. The narrow streets and tightly packed houses might even look familiar to Martin Luther if he were alive today.

During the Renaissance, there was a huge explosion of the arts. Many of the world's well-known artists did their work during the Renaissance. During this time period, artists frequently worked under a sponsor. The sponsor provided support for the artist, who in turn created artwork specifically for their sponsor. The Roman Catholic Church sponsored many great artists, including both Michelangelo and Leonardo da Vinci. As a result, many works of art from this time period depicted religious themes or biblical accounts.

© Shutterstock, Inc.

This depiction of Christ's ascension by an unknown artist demonstrates a painting technique known as fresco. The artist applied pigments mixed with water on a thin layer of wet plaster. As the plaster dried, the pigments reacted with the air to produce the final image.

The father-and-son team of Lucas Cranach the Elder and Lucas Cranach the Younger were two of the most prolific Reformation painters. Their portraits often had religious themes; some portraits were even part of church altars. The portrayals of Bible stories often included contemporary individuals. In the *Raising of Lazarus*, Cranach included images of Martin Luther and Philip Melanchthon as well as some of the German princes.

Reformers' group at a miracle (oil on canvas) by Lucas Cranach, The Younger (1515–86) Nordhausen Cathedral, Nordhausen, Thuringen, Germany/ The Bridgeman Art Library.

One of the interesting things about Cranach portraits is how they mix biblical and contemporary figures. In this portrait of the crucifixion, Cranach portrays the centurion at the foot of the cross as a fifteenth-century knight.

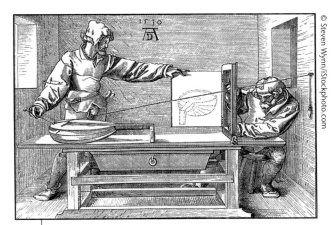

Another art technique perfected during the Reformation was the woodcut. The artist carved a reverse image on a large, flat board. Ink was applied to the carved board and then imprinted on paper to produce the final image. This method allowed the artist to produce multiple copies of the same image. Woodcuts also allowed printers to include pictures in books. Many experts consider Albrecht Dürer the master of the woodcut technique. Dürer produced numerous portraits of people and pictures of Bible stories. This Dürer woodcut shows how Dürer measured and recorded the outlines of objects in order to create his woodcuts. Look for other Dürer woodcuts in this book signed with his initials AD like the ones found at the top of this illustration.

While under the sponsorship of the Pope, Michelangelo used the fresco technique to completely cover the ceiling and one wall of the Sistine Chapel. Each panel of the ceiling depicts a different event from the Book of Genesis. Even the portions of the ceiling that appear to be sculptures are actually painted. Michelangelo took almost four years to complete his work, lying on his back on tall scaffolding.

Sistine Chapel Ceiling, 1508–12 (fresco) (post restoration) by Michelangelo Buonarroti (1475-1564) Vatican Museums and Galleries, Vatican City, Italy/ The Bridgeman Art Library.

Architecture

The simple principle behind the arch changed the way designers and architects thought about buildings. Arches form a self-supporting structure. Each block in the arch transfers its weight to the adjoining block and down to the ground. Over time, architects learned to manipulate the size of the basic building blocks of an arch to create amazing structures.

This interior sketch of a cathedral shows how the arch evolved to allow architects to create incredibly tall and narrow spaces to form the nave (or central aisle) of a cathedral. Notice the series of arches that crisscross each other to form the ceiling. The arches curve downward to join the massive stone columns, which support the weight of the entire building. The arches also allow for the tall windows to bring in light. Over time, most of these large window openings were fitted with stained glass.

This gargoyle on the rooftop of Notre Dame Cathedral is one example of the variety of gargoyles common in Gothic architecture. The fanciful sculptures take many forms, including dragons and other imaginary creatures. But gargoyles are not just decorative, they also function as downspouts to keep rainwater away from the masonry walls of the building.

This structural illustration shows some of the different ways the arch can be used to build a much larger building. The arched window frames let the architect open large areas of the exterior wall, allowing more light into the interior of the building. The exterior arches, called flying buttresses, allow for taller walls and fewer supports on the interior of the building. This made it possible to have larger open areas inside. The strength of the arches working together meant buildings would be stronger and able to hold up for generations. Construction on some of the Gothic cathedrals in Europe began more than nine hundred years ago.

The Cathedral of Notre Dame in Paris displays many of the features seen in the sketch. The use of flying buttress arches allows the cathedral to soar to great heights. Building began on Notre Dame in 1163 on the site of the former Saint Stephen Cathedral, which was first built between the fourth and seventh centuries. Notre Dame continued to be built, remodeled, and rebuilt until it took on its present configuration in 1864, more than seven hundred years after the work began. Improvements and restoration work began again in the late twentieth century.

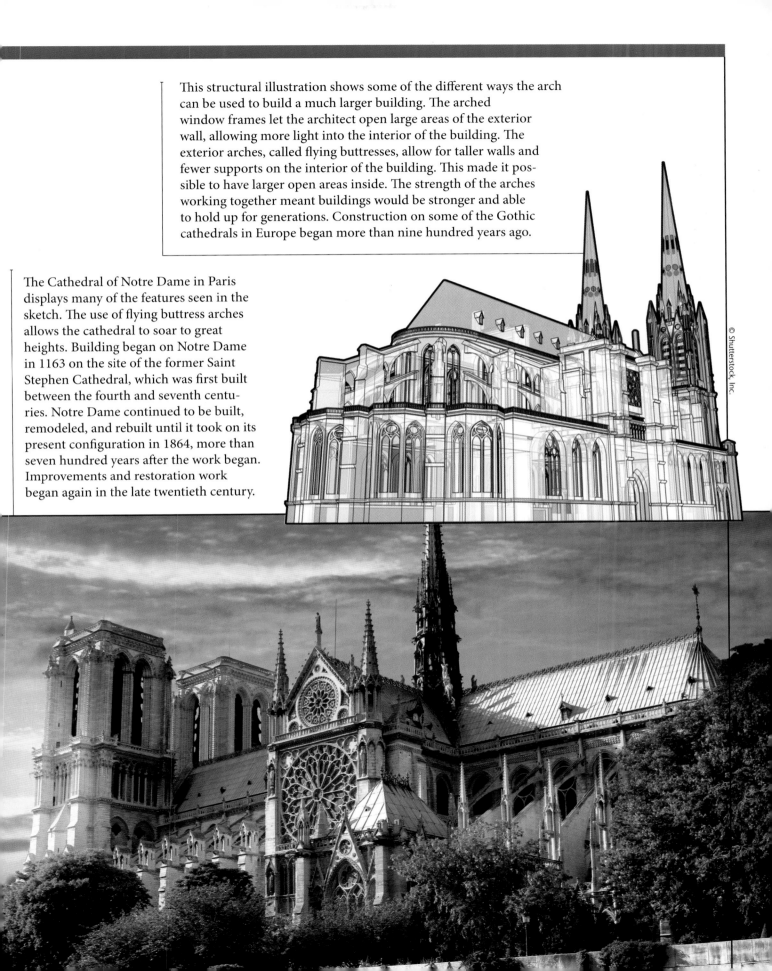

St. Peter's Basilica

■ The papal basilica of Saint Peter in Vatican City is the second-largest church and probably one of the most recognized structures in the world. Historians say the cost of construction set off a series of events leading to the Reformation. Construction on St. Peter's began in 1506 and would continue for the next 120 years.

In this close-up of the sculptures that stand along the front of St. Peter's Basilica, Christ stands at the center with John on one side and Peter on the other.

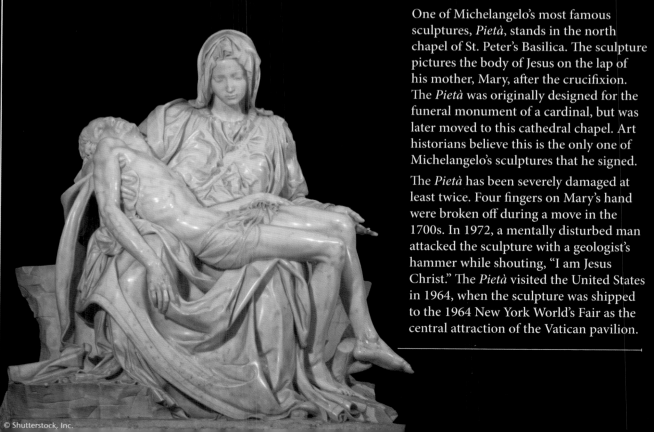

One of Michelangelo's most famous sculptures, *Pietà*, stands in the north chapel of St. Peter's Basilica. The sculpture pictures the body of Jesus on the lap of his mother, Mary, after the crucifixion. The *Pietà* was originally designed for the funeral monument of a cardinal, but was later moved to this cathedral chapel. Art historians believe this is the only one of Michelangelo's sculptures that he signed.

The *Pietà* has been severely damaged at least twice. Four fingers on Mary's hand were broken off during a move in the 1700s. In 1972, a mentally disturbed man attacked the sculpture with a geologist's hammer while shouting, "I am Jesus Christ." The *Pietà* visited the United States in 1964, when the sculpture was shipped to the 1964 New York World's Fair as the central attraction of the Vatican pavilion.

Once construction of the basilica was completed, attention turned to the large plaza in front. An Egyptian obelisk first moved to Rome in AD 37 stood in the center of the open plaza, but there was no connection to the basilica. Designer Giovanni Lorenzo Bernini developed the plan for what is now called St. Peter's Square. The ingenious piazza lined with columns surrounds the plaza and leads visitors visually to the entrance of the basilica.

The high altar of St. Peter's Basilica is topped by an enormous baldachin, or canopy, designed by Bernini. The canopy stands ninety-eight feet tall and is cast entirely of bronze. The twisted columns are said to resemble the columns Jesus was bound to before His crucifixion. The baldachin also helps to bring scale to the interior of the huge dome designed by Michelangelo.

This aerial photo of St. Peter's Square shows the massive size of Bernini's plaza surrounded by the double-columned piazzas.

Indulgences

The massive building project at St. Peter's Basilica drained the financial resources of the Catholic Church. Church leaders needed to raise funds in order to keep the project moving; the sale of indulgences was their solution. Salesmen like Johann Tetzel told the public that the good works of Jesus Christ and the saints had been stored up over the years and could now be distributed in return for a financial contribution. In essence, church leaders took Jesus' free gift of forgiveness and attempted to sell it for profit.

© CPH

A chest like this would have been used to hold money collected through the sale of indulgences. The selling of indulgence led Martin Luther to post his Ninety-five Theses, inviting debate on this practice.

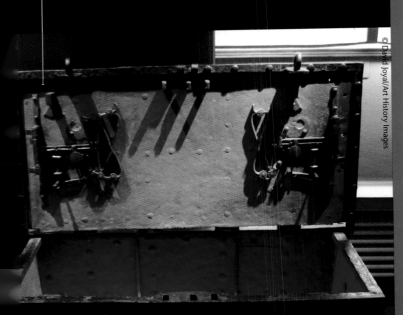

© David Joyal/Art History Images

© bpk, Berlin/Art Resource, NY

Johann Tetzel was appointed to distribute indulgences throughout most of Germany. Tetzel was known for his motivational preaching and creative salesmanship. Tetzel's actions angered many, and leaflets like this one, objecting to the sale of indulgences, soon began to appear.

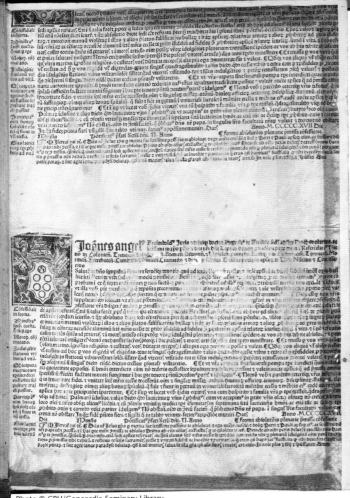

Because paper and velum used for printing were very valuable, printers did not waste misprinted or miscut pages. Instead, they bound these mistakes into other books as the end paper. In 1520, a printer in Wittenberg, Germany, reused misprinted indulgences as the end papers in this volume of Luther's writings.

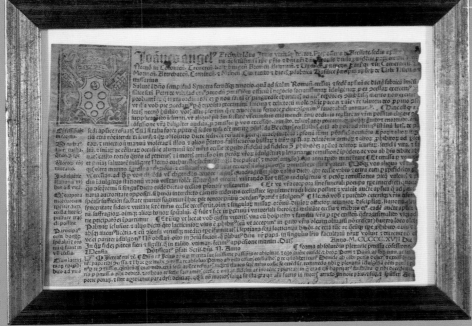

Some original indulgences survive to this day. This unused indulgence from 1517 was found bound inside of a book. Notice the blank spaces in the document where the name of the person granted the indulgence would be filled in by hand. Look carefully in the lower left-hand side of the indulgence for the small pointing-hand icon used to direct the reader's attention to an important point.

Ninety-five Theses

■ On October 31, 1517, a young priest and university professor changed the history of the Church and even the whole world. Martin Luther nailed ninety-five points of discussion to the doors of the Castle Church in Wittenberg. These "theses" addressed what he saw as abuses in the Church (for instance, the sale of indulgences and teachings about purgatory). Luther taught that God's Word was more important than church traditions.

© CPH

The doors of the Castle Church still bear the Ninety-five Theses today. The original wooden doors were destroyed by fire and replaced by these bronze doors with the words of Luther's Ninety-five Theses engraved on them.

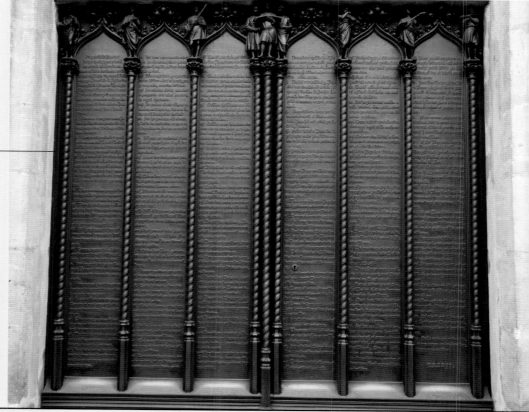

© Andreas Kaspar/iStockphoto.com

© David Joyal/Art History Images

As the Reformation spread, Castle Church embraced Luther's reforms. Following his death on February 18, 1546, Luther's body was returned from Eisleben, Germany, to Wittenberg. Luther was buried here beneath the pulpit of the Castle Church because it was said that his most important work took place in the pulpit, where he clearly taught the Word of God.

© The Bridgeman Art Library

This woodcut cartoon from the time of the Reformation contains a number of interesting scenes. On the far right, we see Elector Frederick the Wise sleeping and dreaming the rest of the scenes in the print. On the far left, Luther is pictured writing his Ninety-five Theses on the Castle Church doors. The other end of Luther's pen stretches all the way to Rome, where it pokes Johann Tetzel and the pope. In the background, we see Martin Luther reading his Bible, which he taught was the only source for teaching and doctrine.

Rulers and Princes

Government structure during the Renaissance and Reformation was very different from today. The emperor ruled a large area with princes under him. The emperor might be appointed by church leaders or inherit his position from a relative. Elections and democratic principles as used today did not exist.

This bronze sculpture depicts Charles V, emperor of the Holy Roman Empire during the Reformation. Charles hosted the Diet at Augsburg in hopes of discrediting the reformers and keeping the peace among the German princes.

© Shutterstock, Inc.

This stained-glass shield from Kyburg Castle in Zurich, Switzerland, displays a royal crest surrounded by city shields. At the time of the Reformation, many cities had their own rulers. The shields used symbols representing the ruling family of the city. Each image in the shield had a special meaning. The crown represented royalty, lions symbolized bravery and valor, bears represented strength or cunning, and twin-headed eagles symbolized protection.

Electors of Saxony: Frederick the Wise (1486–1525), John the Steadfast (1468–1532), and John Frederick the Magnanimous (1503–54). 1532 (oil on panel) by Lucas Cranach, the Elder (1472–1553) Hamburger Kunsthalle. Hamburg, Germany/The Bridgeman Art Library.

© Fedor Selivanov/Shutterstock, Inc.

© Duncan Walker/iStockphoto.com

This three-panel portrait by Lucas Cranach the Elder in 1532 shows the electors of Saxony during the Reformation. Frederick the Wise (1463–1525) on the left started the University of Wittenberg and was responsible for appointing Martin Luther and Philip Melanchthon to their professorships. Frederick also arranged for Luther to be "kidnapped" and taken to the safety of Wartburg Castle following the Diet of Worms.

The center panel shows John the Steadfast (1468–1532), Frederick's brother, who continued Frederick's policies and helped the early reformed church grow.

John Frederick the Magnanimous (1503–1554), on the right, was the son of John the Steadfast; John Frederick was educated by one of Luther's advisors and friends. John Frederick corresponded with Luther and became a regular student of Luther's writings.

CHARLEMAGNE

This engraving by Albrecht Dürer portrays Charlemagne, the king of the Franks and later the Holy Roman Emperor. His richly detailed robes and crown would typically only be worn for ceremonial occasions. In one hand, he holds an orb representing his role as Holy Roman Emperor. The cross on the globe symbolizes the rule of Christ over the whole world. The two shields at the top portray the countries at the heart of Charlemagne's kingdom, Germany (the eagle) and France (the fleur-de-lis).

Silencing Luther

The Roman Catholic Church was not happy with Martin Luther and his Ninety-five Theses. They tried to silence Luther, and for a while, Luther agreed to keep silent as long as church leaders kept silent as well. But Catholic church leaders soon broke the silence and tried to criticize Luther further. Eventually, the pope issued a special document, called a "bull," threatening Luther with excommunication if he did not take back some of what the pope considered false teaching. Luther's enemies began to burn Luther's books and pamphlets. In response, Luther hosted his own bonfire, where he burned many books of Catholic law and writings of Catholic church leaders. Luther then topped off the blaze by adding a copy of the bull he received from the pope.

Photo © CPH

Probably the most-often quoted words of Martin Luther, "Here I stand," were spoken at the Diet of Worms. The Diet was a meeting of religious leaders held in Worms, Germany. Charles V arranged this conference so church leaders could question Luther about his teachings. When pressured to recant or give up his teachings, Luther asked for time to consider his answer. When the same question was asked the next day, Luther went through his books explaining that if someone could show him how his writings were incorrect based on the Bible, he would burn the books himself. Still not satisfied, the emperor pressed Luther further. Finally, Luther replied:

> Unless I am convinced by the testimony of the Scriptures or by clear reason . . . , I am bound by the Scriptures I have quoted and my conscience is captive to the Word of God. I cannot and I will not retract anything, since it is neither safe nor right to go against conscience. I cannot do otherwise, here I stand, may God help me, Amen.

Photo ©

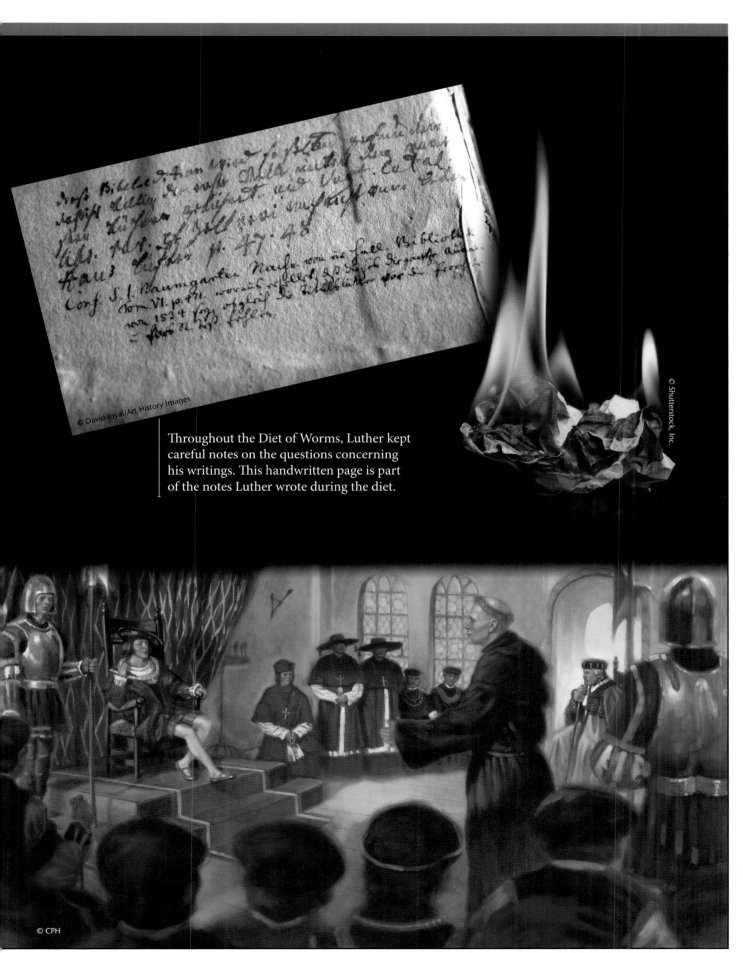

© David Joyal/Art History Images

© Shutterstock, Inc.

Throughout the Diet of Worms, Luther kept careful notes on the questions concerning his writings. This handwritten page is part of the notes Luther wrote during the diet.

© CPH

Knights

- Knights worked for noblemen to protect their property and enforce the laws. A knight depended on different kinds of armor and weapons for protection.

This set of Spanish armor is actually from a time after the Reformation. The breastplate protected the soldier's vital organs while the helmet protected his head. Both pieces of armor are heavily engraved.

© Shutterstock, Inc.

© Henk Bentlage/Shutterstock, Inc.

© Shutterstock, Inc.

Knights used horses to travel from place to place and in battle. This knight wears chain mail formed by linking together thousands of small, overlapping metal rings. Chain mail was very heavy but allowed for greater freedom of movement than sheet-metal armor. Chain mail was used to protect the body while a helmet, chest protection, and gloves covered other vital body parts. The knight's brightly colored clothing and insignia helped identify who he fought for, much like how uniforms identify teams today.

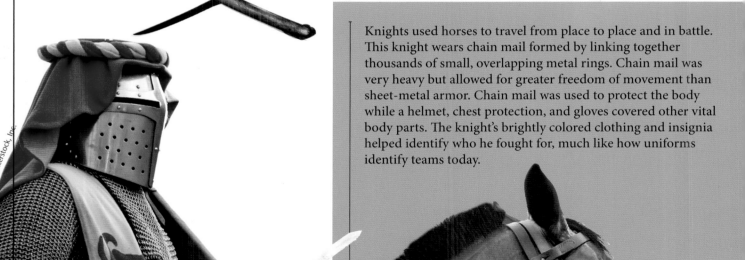

This medieval helmet shows the careful construction designed to protect the knight. The heavy trim along the nose and around the eyeholes provides added strength where the user needs extra protection. The wide eyeholes allow the knight to scan the battlefield without having to turn his head.

© Shutterstock, Inc.

Knights not only had very real enemies, but they also faced temptations and dangers every day. This woodcut by artist Dürer, first printed in 1513, shows a knight on horseback pursued by Death and the Devil.

Protecting your hands was very important for the knight. These armored gloves, made of many separate pieces of metal joined carefully together, allowed the wearer to move their hands easily while still being fully protected. The long cuffs protected the knight's wrists from sword or dagger blows.

Courtesy: Yale University

In addition to protective armor, a knight needs weapons to use in battle. The pointed tips and curved blades were put on long poles called "pikes." In the hands of an experienced knight, a pike could unseat and severely injure a knight on horseback.

Wartburg

Following the Diet of Worms, Martin Luther became a wanted man. Luther's friend Frederick the Wise arranged for Martin to "disappear." While traveling along the road to Wittenberg, Luther and his companions were suddenly surrounded by armed horsemen. They captured Luther, who wisely grabbed his Hebrew Bible and Greek New Testament before being led away. The captors put Luther in a cell at the nearly deserted Wartburg Castle; not even Frederick the Wise knew exactly where his men had taken Luther.

© Enrico Agostoni/Shutterstoc

© iStockphoto.com

While in hiding at Wartburg, Luther let his hair and beard grow while calling himself "Knight George" (Junker Jörg). This portrait by Lucas Cranach shows Luther's very different appearance while in hiding.

Luther used his time in hiding to continue reforming the Church. He wrote a number of books and pamphlets, which were taken to a printer and distributed throughout Germany. But Luther's biggest project would change the way everyone approached the Bible. He carefully began translating the New Testament from Greek into German. Finally, people could read God's Word in their own language!

© M. Wolf/Shutterstock, Inc.

Wartburg Castle was built on a mountainside overlooking the town of Eisenach, Germany. The first sections of the castle date to 1067 with some sections built as late as the nineteenth century. Each section demonstrates the style of architecture popular at the time it was constructed. More than once, the castle has fallen into ruin only to be rebuilt by later generations. While Eisenach was bombed heavily during World War II, Wartburg was spared any major damage. Now listed as a UNESCO (United Nations Educational, Scientific, and Cultural Organization) World Heritage Site, tourists from around the world visit Wartburg every year.

Martin Luther completed his translation of the New Testament during his captivity. Later, together with Philip Melanchthon and others, he finished translating the entire Bible into German.

Luther (1483–1589), Melanchthon (1497–1560), Pomeranus (1485–1558), and Cruciger (1508–48) translating the Bible (engraving) by English School (19th century) Private Collection/Ken Welsh/The Bridgeman Art Library.

Peasants' War

TOMAS MVNCER PREDIGER ZV ALSTET IN DVRINGEN.

Thomas Müntzer became one of the outspoken leaders of the Peasants' Revolt (1524–1525). Luther told the peasants to respect their leaders, but Müntzer told peasants to ignore Luther, destroy the noblemen's property, and kill the wicked princes and priests. Over forty monasteries and castles in the central part of Germany were destroyed by the angry peasants. Müntzer was finally captured at a battle in Mühlhausen while hiding in bed. He was tried and executed for his role in leading the rebellion.

Thomas Müntzer, c 1600 (hand colored woodcut) by German School Private Collection/ The Bridgeman Art Library.

Few peasants in Germany owned the land they farmed. The land was controlled by powerful noblemen and the Catholic Church. The peasants attempted to revolt a number of times, but this time, some peasants were trying to use Luther's words and writings as an excuse to overturn the powerful nobles. Armed with common farm implements and torches, the peasants were ready for war.

When Martin Luther found out the peasants were using his writings to justify the revolt, he tried to preach against their actions. Those who disagreed with Luther even heckled him during a sermon he preached against the revolt.

Luther wrote a tract, *Against the Murderous and Thieving Hordes of Peasants*, when he returned home to Wittenberg. Luther was disappointed, and many people objected to his angry words in the tract, which actually came out after the peasants had been overthrown by soldiers working for the nobles.

Philip Melanchthon served at Wittenberg University with Martin Luther, whom Melanchthon often called his "spiritual father." Melanchthon was especially interested in the writings of Paul, and his commitment to the study of the Scriptures led to his appointment to the theological faculty at Wittenberg.

1526

VIVENTIS·POTVIT·DVRERIVS·ORA·PHILIPPI
MENTEM·NON·POTVIT·PINGERE·DOCTA
MANVS

© Duncan Walker/iStockphoto.com

228
PHILIPPVS MELANTHON,
maniæ Phœnix.

Paruus eram: necme tamen ingens cepit hic orbis:
Fama mei complet nominis omne latus.

M. D. LX.

Photo © CPH/Concordia Seminary Library

Photo © CPH

Martin Luther translated the New Testament into German in a matter of months while in hiding at Wartburg. Old Testament Hebrew would prove to be a greater challenge. The full translation of the Old Testament would take twelve years. Philip Melanchthon stepped up to help Luther work through the task of translating the Scriptures into the language of the people.

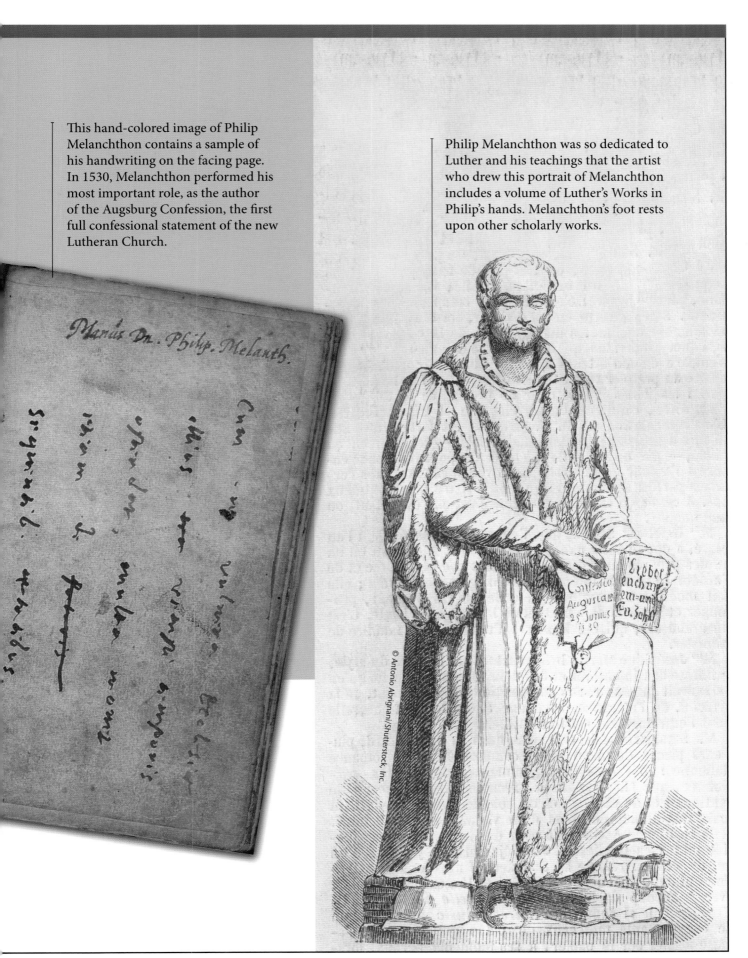

This hand-colored image of Philip Melanchthon contains a sample of his handwriting on the facing page. In 1530, Melanchthon performed his most important role, as the author of the Augsburg Confession, the first full confessional statement of the new Lutheran Church.

Philip Melanchthon was so dedicated to Luther and his teachings that the artist who drew this portrait of Melanchthon includes a volume of Luther's Works in Philip's hands. Melanchthon's foot rests upon other scholarly works.

■ Martin Luther and his followers faced increasing pressure to defend their beliefs. One Catholic leader, John Eck, wrote a book listing over four hundred "errors" in Luther's teachings. However, Eck included teachings from other reformers, things Luther never said. Now, Emperor Charles V called a meeting of the Lutheran princes in Augsburg. Philip Melanchthon stepped forward to draft a new summary of Lutheran teachings. Rather than defend against false accusations, Melanchthon wrote a thorough explanation of Lutheran teachings, called the Augsburg Confession.

At the Diet of Augsburg, the Catholic princes wrote a response to the Augsburg Confession called the Confutation, but they refused to give the Lutheran leaders a copy of the document. Thankfully, the secretaries for the Lutheran princes took great notes as the Confutation was read, and the Lutheran leaders wrote a response called The Apology (or "defense") of the Augsburg Confession. The Apology joined the Augsburg Confession in the Book of Concord.

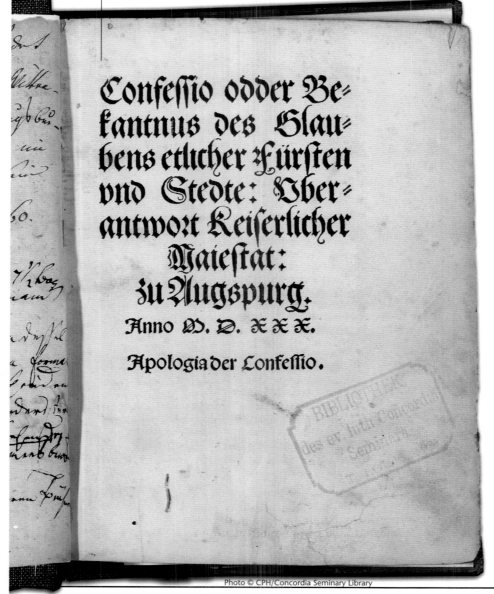

Photo CPH

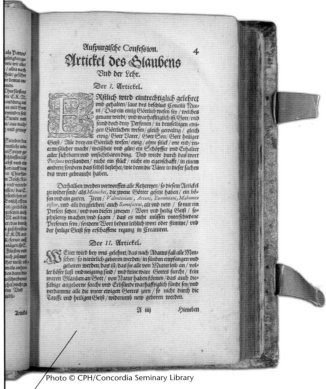

Despite the objections of Charles V and the Catholic princes, the Augsburg Confession became the standard of beliefs for the Lutheran Church. Elector John and the Lutheran princes stood their ground and signed the Augsburg Confession as their official statement of beliefs. Eventually, the Augsburg Confession joined other confessional documents and was published in this *Book of Concord* in 1580.

Katharina Luther

Katharina von Bora was one of twelve nuns who escaped from the cloister in Marienthron. Katie was a sensible, hard-working young woman.

© iStockphoto.com

© Olga Millan Anoro/Shutterstock, Inc. and © iStockphoto.com

In 1523, Luther helped twelve nuns escape from a cloister; they hid in the back of a wagon full of empty herring barrels. Late on Easter Eve, the nuns stowed away in the barrels until they reached the safety of a neighboring town. Three nuns returned to their family homes, while Luther worked to find jobs or homes for the remaining nine.

Two years after the nuns' escape from the cloister, Luther managed to find suitable husbands for eight of the escaped nuns. But Katharina von Bora remained unmarried despite two attempts to find her a spouse. Finally, Luther decided that perhaps he should marry Katie himself—so on June 13, 1525, Martin and Katie married.

Martin and Katie grew in their love for each other throughout their nearly twenty-one years together as husband and wife. Luther often called his wife "Kitty, my rib" as a reminder of how Eve was taken from Adam's rib. These carved ivory busts from the eighteenth century fold together in a small leather box. This type of carving might have been a souvenir for someone visiting Germany.

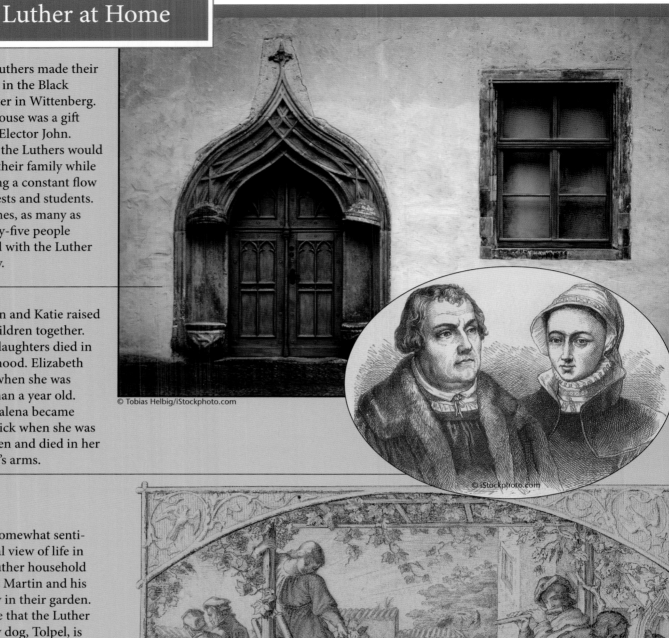

The Luthers made their home in the Black Cloister in Wittenberg. The house was a gift from Elector John. Here, the Luthers would raise their family while hosting a constant flow of guests and students. At times, as many as twenty-five people stayed with the Luther family.

Martin and Katie raised six children together. Two daughters died in childhood. Elizabeth died when she was less than a year old. Magdalena became very sick when she was thirteen and died in her father's arms.

© Tobias Helbig/iStockphoto.com

iStockphoto.com

This somewhat sentimental view of life in the Luther household shows Martin and his family in their garden. Notice that the Luther family dog, Tolpel, is even included in the picture. Katie kept four gardens and also ran the family farm that she bought with the help of Elector John. The family raised cows, pigs, goats, chickens, geese, and doves. Katie even learned to brew her own beer.

© CPH

Luther's family celebrates Christmas in this illustration. Some historians credit Martin Luther for bringing evergreen trees into homes as part of the Christmas celebration.

Many students and scholars spent time with Luther and his family. One scholar, Johann Reiffenstein, drew this sketch of Luther as he presented one of his last lectures. The notes surrounding the sketch were written by Melanchthon: "Living, I was your menace; dying, I will be your death, pope. In the year of 1546, leaving his 63rd year behind while entering his 64th year, he died. And though he may be dead—he lives!"

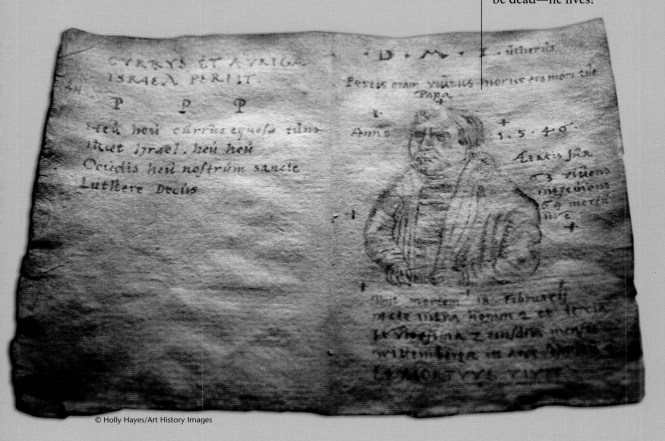

The twin towers mark the City Church, or St. Mary's Church, in Wittenberg. First built in the thirteenth century, City Church became the first church to have mass in the German language. Many consider this congregation the "mother church" of the Reformation.

© Christina Hanck/iStockphoto.com

© Christina Hanck/iStockphoto.com

To help organize worship in the newly formed church, Martin Luther studied the Roman Catholic Mass and made revisions. First, he encouraged the use of German in the service. Revised liturgies emphasized the Gospel message and helped worshipers focus on Christ. Congregations were encouraged to sing more hymns as a way of teaching and learning the doctrine of the Church. The German Mass was completed and used for the first time on Christmas Day 1525 at City Church; it was published the next month.

Deudsche Messe vnd ordnung Gottis diensts.

Wittemberg.

Photo © CPH/Concordia Seminary Library

Martin Luther made the sermon a major part of
the worship service in the newly reformed Church.
Luther was considered such an impressive preacher,
the elector arranged to have Luther buried beneath
the pulpit of Castle Church when he died.

Photo © CPH

One of the major changes Martin Luther made in the
celebration of the mass was giving both the bread and the
wine to participants in Holy Communion. At this time,
the Roman Catholic Church reserved the wine for priests
only. From his study of the Scriptures, Luther knew that
the gift of Christ's body and blood was for all believers.
The importance of the Sacrament of Holy Communion
continues to set the Lutheran Church apart from others.

© CPH

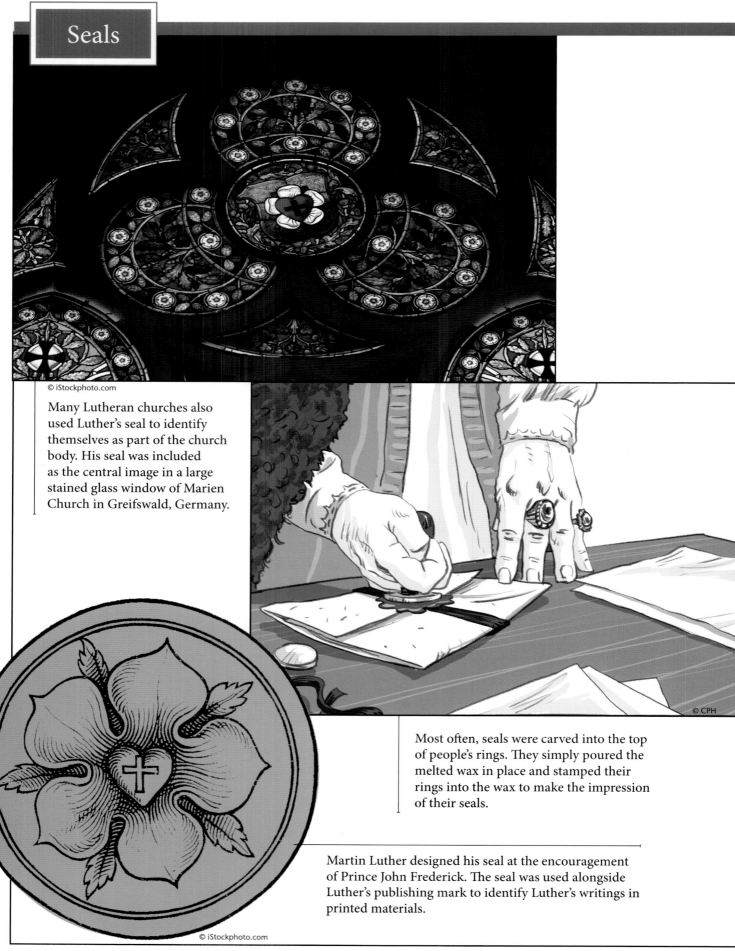

© iStockphoto.com

Many Lutheran churches also used Luther's seal to identify themselves as part of the church body. His seal was included as the central image in a large stained glass window of Marien Church in Greifswald, Germany.

© CPH

Most often, seals were carved into the top of people's rings. They simply poured the melted wax in place and stamped their rings into the wax to make the impression of their seals.

Martin Luther designed his seal at the encouragement of Prince John Frederick. The seal was used alongside Luther's publishing mark to identify Luther's writings in printed materials.

© iStockphoto.com

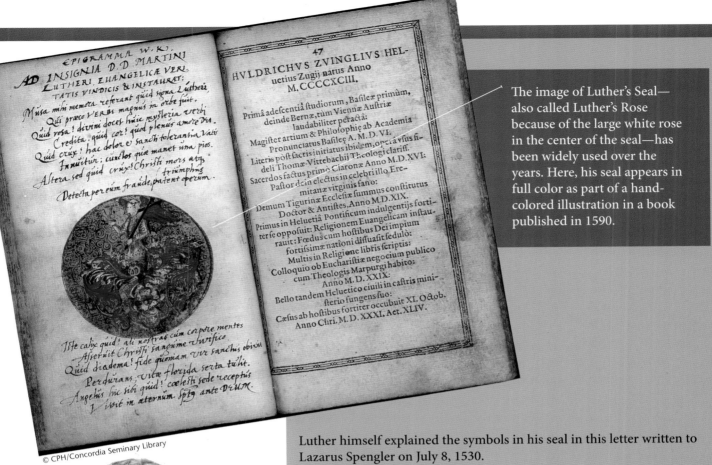

EPIGRAMMA W.K.
AD INSIGNIA D.D. MARTINI
LUTHERI EVANGELICÆ VERI-
TATIS VINDICIS & INSTAURAT:

Musa mihi memora referant quid signa Lutheri,
Qui præco VERBI magnus in orbe fuit,
Quid rosa! divine doces huic mysteria verbi,
Credita, quid cor? quid plenus amore Dei.
Quid crux! hac dolor & sancti tolerantia Vatis
Innuitur; cunctos quæ manet una pios.
Altera sed quid crux! triumphus
Detecta per eum fraude, patent operum.

Iste calix quid! ali nostras cum corpore mentes
Asseruit Christi sanguine Iunifico.
Quid diadema! fide quoniam vir sanctus obivit
Perdurans; vita florida serta tulit.
Angelis hic sibi quid! coelesti sede receptis
Vivit in æternum sptg ante DEUM.

47

HVLDRICHVS ZVINGLIVS HEL-
uetius Zugij natus Anno
M.CCCCXCIII.

Primâ adefcentiâ ftudiorum, Bafileæ primùm,
deinde Bernæ, tùm Viennæ Auftriæ
laudabiliter peractâ:
Magifter artium & Philofophiæ ab Academia
Pronunciatus Bafileæ A. M. D. VI.
Literis pôft factis initiatus ibidem, operâ vfus fi-
deli Thomæ-Vittebachij Theologi clariff.
Sacerdos factus primô Claronæ Anno M.D.XVI:
Paftor dein electus in celebri illo Ere-
mitanæ virginis fano:
Demum Tigurinæ Ecclefiæ fummus conftitutus
Doctor & Antiftes, Anno M.D.XIX.
Primus in Heluetiâ Pontificum indulgentiâ forti-
ter fe oppofuit: Religionem Euangelicam inftau-
rauit: Fœdus cum hoftibus Dei impium
fortifimæ nationi diffuafit fedulô:
Multis in Religione libris fcriptis:
Colloquio ob Euchariftiæ negocium publico
cum Theologis Marpurgi habito:
Anno M. D. XXIX.
Bello tandem Heluetico ciuili in caftris mini-
fterio fungens fuo:
Cæfus ab hoftibus fortiter occubuit XI. Octob.
Anno Chri. M. D. XXXI. Act. XLIV.

© CPH/Concordia Seminary Library

The image of Luther's Seal—also called Luther's Rose because of the large white rose in the center of the seal—has been widely used over the years. Here, his seal appears in full color as part of a hand-colored illustration in a book published in 1590.

In this time, important documents and letters were sent by messenger, often on horseback. In order to keep the contents secret, seals were used to close the letter or package. The sender used a string to tie the parcel shut and sealed the ends of the string with melted wax. Finally, the sender made an imprint of his or her seal in the soft wax.

Luther himself explained the symbols in his seal in this letter written to Lazarus Spengler on July 8, 1530.

Grace and peace in Christ!

Honorable, kind, dear Sir and Friend! Since you ask whether my seal has come out correctly, I shall answer most amiably and tell you of those thoughts which [now] come to my mind about my seal as a symbol of my theology.

There is first to be a cross, black [and placed] in a heart, which should be of its natural color, so that I myself would be reminded that faith in the Crucified saves us. For if one believes from the heart he will be justified. Even though it is a black cross, [which] mortifies and [which] also should hurt us, yet it leaves the heart in its [natural] color [and] does not ruin nature; that is, [the cross] does not kill but keeps [man] alive. For the just man lives by faith, but by faith in the Crucified One. Such a heart is to be in the midst of a white rose, to symbolize that faith gives joy, comfort, and peace; in a word it places the believer into a white joyful rose; for [this faith] does not give peace and joy as the world gives and, therefore, the rose is to be white and not red, for white is the color of the spirits and of all the angels. Such a rose is to be in a sky-blue field, [symbolizing] that such joy in the Spirit and in faith is a beginning of the future heavenly joy; it is already a part [of faith], and is grasped through hope, even though not yet manifest. And around this field is a golden ring, [symbolizing] that in heaven such blessedness lasts forever and has no end, and in addition is precious beyond all joy and goods, just as gold is the most valuable and precious metal.

May Christ, our dear Lord, be with your spirit until the life to come. Amen.

■ Many historians credit the invention of movable type and the printing press as one of the most influential inventions of all time. Martin Luther's writings as well as the writings of other reformers spread rapidly because the printing press made it possible to print multiple copies quickly. As a result, Reformation literature spread throughout Europe.

Johannes Gutenberg started using moveable type as early as 1439. He combined moveable type, the printing press, and oil-based ink to mass produce books. His major life's work was producing printed copies of the Bible.

© iStockphoto.com

© iStockphoto.com

Above is a close-up of an early printing press showing the huge wooden screw used to apply pressure to the type plate and create the printed image.

AND in the. l. yere vppon the euen of Sainct Thomas the Apostle before Christmas , was yelden by appoint mente, the castle of Kenelworthe. At the whiche the king with his power had line, as before is said,

© Kenneth V. Pilon/Shutterstock, Inc.

This sample of a printed page shows how moveable type allowed different sizes and styles of type to appear on the same page. The large letter A with the decorative designs would be a single type block; the rest of the text was formed from individual pieces of type.

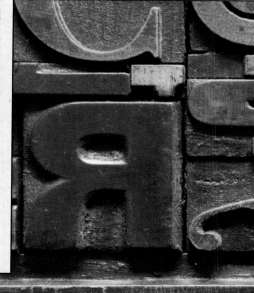

© Shutterstock, Inc.

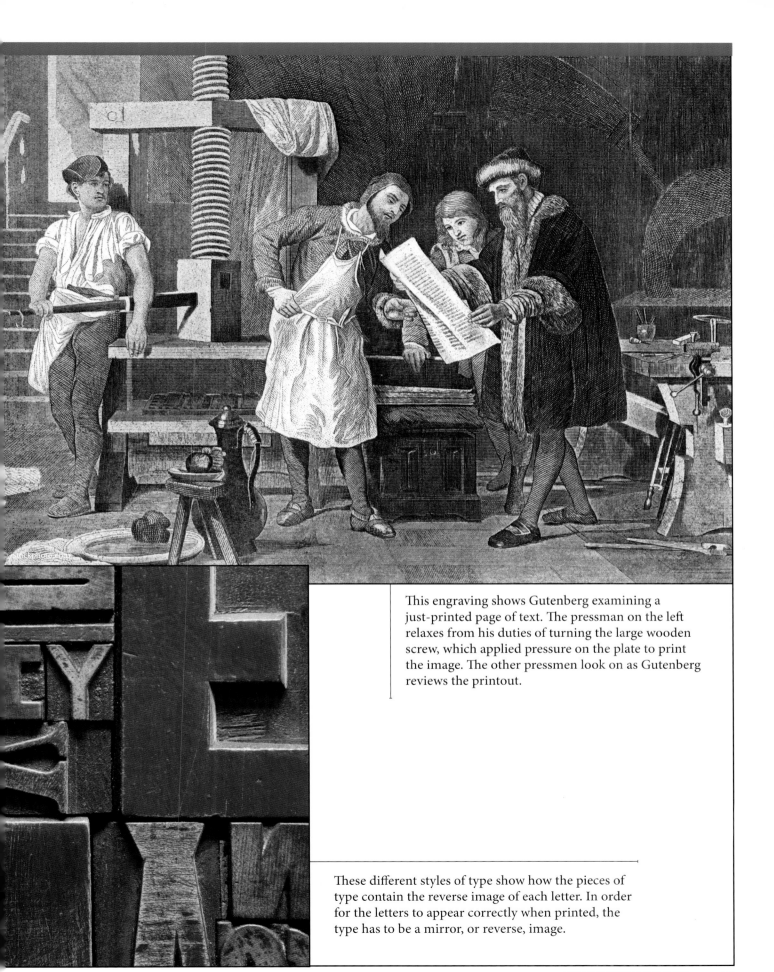

This engraving shows Gutenberg examining a just-printed page of text. The pressman on the left relaxes from his duties of turning the large wooden screw, which applied pressure on the plate to print the image. The other pressmen look on as Gutenberg reviews the printout.

These different styles of type show how the pieces of type contain the reverse image of each letter. In order for the letters to appear correctly when printed, the type has to be a mirror, or reverse, image.

This early engraving shows Hans Lufft, the printer who produced Luther's German Bible. Lufft's printing mark appears in the upper left-hand side of the engraving. Lufft played a major role in spreading the Reformation by printing Luther's writings.

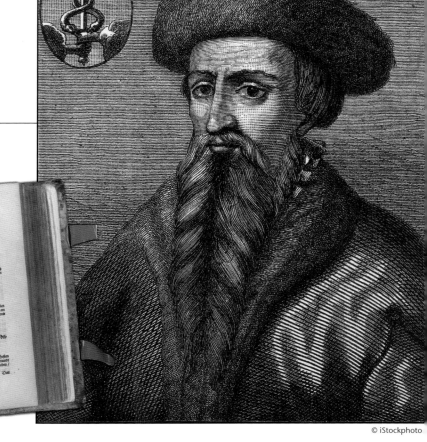

© iStockphoto

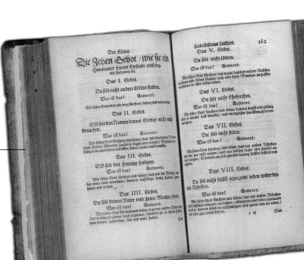

Photo © CPH/Concordia Seminary Library

Martin Luther wanted to provide churches and families with resources to help teach the faith. A series of sermons Luther preached in 1528 provided the basic content of the Large Catechism. The Large Catechism appeared in April 1529 and the Small Catechism one month later. This two-page spread from the Book of Concord shows the Ten Commandments as they appeared in the Small Catechism.

These two cover pages, from Luther's book *The Word of Christ* (on right) and Luther's German Mass (left), show how the printer reused the engraved plate with the images of deer and winged creatures. The type in the center was simply changed to print the text to go with the appropriate book.

Photo © CPH/Concordia Seminary Library

Before the Diet of Augsburg, Luther wrote materials called *postils* (which were gathered into pamphlets) to help pastors prepare sermons. Later, students took notes on Luther's sermons, which were released in bound volumes, such as this collection of sermons based on Matthew 8.

Martin Luther completed his first complete German Bible in 1534; he continued to make corrections and adjustments until 1544. This cover page from a 1652 edition of Luther's German Bible was printed in Nuremberg, Germany.

The cover of the Bible is wood, covered with leather and accented with metal corners and clasps designed to help protect the Bible. The clasps helped hold the Bible closed when it was moved. This edition of the German Bible is approximately twenty-four inches tall and about eighteen inches thick.

© iStockphoto.com

John Calvin, on the left of this engraving, was born into a Roman Catholic family with the means to have him well educated. Calvin led a major effort to reform the church and society in Geneva, Switzerland. Calvin and Luther could not agree on key points of theology, especially predestination and the Sacraments. Calvin is considered the father of the Reformed Church.

Ulrich Zwingli, on the right, was a Swiss reformer who led the Reformation in Switzerland. Like Calvin, he severely disagreed with Luther on issues surrounding the Sacraments of Baptism and Communion. Zwingli was killed in a battle between Catholics and Protestants in 1531. Legend has it that Zwingli had his body quartered, burned, and mixed with dung to prevent his remains from becoming relics.

© iStockphoto.com

The Scottish reformer John Knox lived 1514–1572. Trained as a Roman Catholic priest, he left the Catholic Church and studied with Calvin and other reformers before returning to Scotland to lead the reformation of the church there. Today, Knox is considered the founder of the Presbyterian Church.

This allegorical representation of the pope and the Reformation from about 1520 shows the "house" of the church in a run-down state and under attack by reformers while the pope and bishops escape by climbing the roof. When Luther posted his Ninety-five Theses, he had not intended to create a new church, only to correct those teachings opposed to the Word of God.

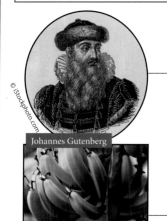

Johannes Gutenberg
© iStockphoto.com

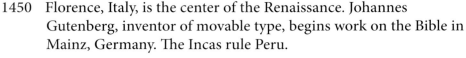

© Rachel Sardo/iStockphoto.com

© Shutterstock, Inc.

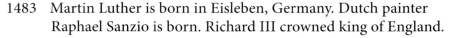

© Anna Yu /iStockphoto.com

Henry VIII
© Duncan Walker /
iStockphoto.com

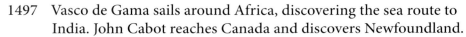

Copernicus
© Ray Roper/
iStockphoto.com

Martin Luther
© CPH

1450 Florence, Italy, is the center of the Renaissance. Johannes Gutenberg, inventor of movable type, begins work on the Bible in Mainz, Germany. The Incas rule Peru.

1453 The Turks conquer Constantinople.

1455 Wars of the Roses begin in England. Gutenberg prints his first Bible.

1462 Ivan the Great rules Russia.

1480 Ferdinand Magellan is born in Portugal. The Spanish Inquisition begins.

1482 Portuguese explorers bring bananas from the coast of Africa to their plantations.

1483 Martin Luther is born in Eisleben, Germany. Dutch painter Raphael Sanzio is born. Richard III crowned king of England.

1484 Ulrich Zwingli, future reformer in Switzerland, is born.

1485 Leonardo da Vinci studies flight, starting sketches for the parachute as well as the inspiration for the modern-day helicopter.

1492 Columbus becomes the first European to encounter the Caribbean. Jews are driven out of Spain.

1497 Vasco de Gama sails around Africa, discovering the sea route to India. John Cabot reaches Canada and discovers Newfoundland.

1498 Da Vinci paints *The Last Supper*.

1500 Portuguese navigator Pedro Alvares Cabral discovers Brazil.

1501 Louis XII conquers Italy. Michelangelo Buonarroti begins to sculpt *David*.

1502 First black slaves arrive in America at the Spanish colony of Santo Domingo.

1503 Da Vinci begins to paint the *Mona Lisa*.

1506 St. Peter's Basilica in Rome is started. Christopher Columbus dies.

1507 Smallpox affects Hispaniola, the first reported outbreak in the New World.

1508 Michelangelo begins painting the Sistine Chapel.

1509 Henry VIII is crowned king of England.

1510 Luther travels to Rome. England is struck by the "great plague."

1512 Ponce de Leon claims Florida for Spain. Nicolaus Copernicus proposes that the sun is the center of the solar system.

1517 Luther posts his Ninety-five Theses.

1519   Zwingli begins Protestant Reformation in Switzerland. Hernán Cortés explores Mexico. Charles I becomes the Holy Roman Emperor as Charles V. Magellan sets out to circumnavigate the globe. Da Vinci dies.

1520   Süleyman becomes sultan of Turkey.

1521   Luther is excommunicated. Magellan is killed in the Philippines; the remaining crew completes the journey and returns to Spain in 1522. The Ottomans conquer Belgrade.

1522   New Testament is published in German.

1524   Peasants' War begins in southern Germany. Giovanni da Verrazano explores the New England coast and New York Bay.

1527   Pope Clement VII is imprisoned and the Italian Renaissance ends. The Protestant Reformation begins in Sweden.

1529   The Ottomans are defeated in Vienna by the Austrian army.

1531   The Inca civil war is fought.

1532   Francisco Pizarro defeats the Incas in Peru.

1533   Henry VIII marries Anne Boleyn, his second wife, and is excommunicated by the pope.

1534   Henry VIII makes himself head of the Church of England. Jacques Cartier claims Quebec for France. The Ottomans capture Bagdad. German Bible is published.

1535   Cartier sails up the St. Lawrence River and claims all of Canada for France. Sir Thomas More is executed.

1536   Henry VIII has his wife Anne Boleyn executed so he can marry Jane Seymour. John Calvin establishes the Reformed and Presbyterian form of Protestantism in Switzerland. The Spanish Inquisition begins in Portugal.

1539   Hernando de Soto explores inland North America. Juan Pablos begins printing in Mexico.

1540   Thomas Cromwell is executed.

1542   Francisco de Orellana discovers the Amazon. De Soto explores the Mississippi River. Portuguese traders land in China.

1543   Copernicus's theory of planetary orbit is published.

1545   Council of Trent meets to define Catholic dogma.

1546   Luther dies.

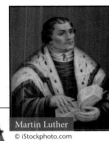

Martin Luther
© iStockphoto.com

Photo © CPH/
Concordia Seminary
Library

© iStockphoto.com

Anne Boleyn
© iStockphoto.com

© Duncan Walker / iStockphoto.com

Thomas Cromwell

John Knox
© iStockphoto.com

Ivan the Terrible
© Duncan Walker/
iStockphoto.com

Mary I
© Steven Wynn/iStockphoto.com

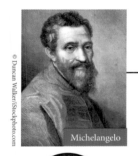

© Duncan Walker/iStockphoto.com

Michelangelo

Francis Drake
© Duncan Walker/iStockphoto.com

1547 John Knox leads the Protestant Reformation and establishes the Presbyterian Church in Scotland. Ivan the Terrible is crowned tsar of Russia.

1553 Mary I becomes queen, begins to restore Roman Catholicism in England.

1554 Portuguese missionaries establish Sao Paulo in Brazil.

1555 First major joint stock trading company in England.

1556 First music book is printed in the New World. History's deadliest earthquake strikes Shaanxi, China.

1558 Queen Elizabeth I ascends to the throne in England and restores Protestantism. This begins the English Renaissance, influencing commerce, politics, and the arts (involving William Shakespeare, Christopher Marlowe, and Edmund Spenser).

1561 Persecution of Huguenots in France ends, until about a decade later when the French religious wars begin again.

1564 Michelangelo dies.

1565 Rio de Janeiro is founded.

1570 Queen Elizabeth I excommunicated by Pope Pius V.

1571 Manila is founded.

1580 Francis Drake returns to England after circumnavigating the globe.

1582 Gregorian calendar is implemented.

1587 Mary, queen of Scots, is executed.

1588 Spanish Armada is defeated.

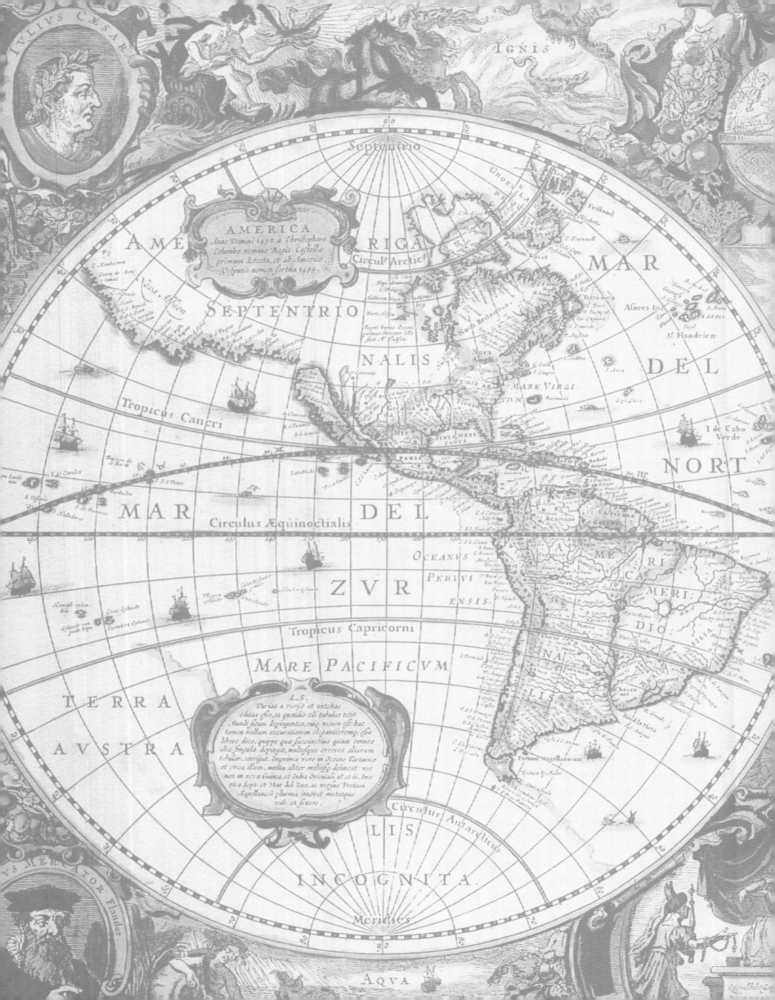